THE FORM BOOK

THE ULTIMATE GUIDE TO THE BRITISH NIGHT OUT

Kyle Lightning

The Form Book - First Addition

Copyright © [2023] [Kyle Lightning]
SnapThis

Self Published

Safety Warning:
This book is designed to help you have a fun and safe night out, but it is important to remember that drinking should always be done responsibly and within your limits. The information provided in this book is not an invite to drink excessively or engage in risky behavior.

We strongly advise you to take responsibility for your own safety and the safety of those around you. Always stay aware of your surroundings and trust your instincts. If at any point during the night you feel uncomfortable or unsafe, leave the situation immediately.

KYLE LIGHTNING

ISBN: 9798389350502

Art Cover - @oliviaprodesign
Illustrations - @FizzingClouds

Created in the United Kingdom

KYLE LIGHTNING

THE FORM BOOK

THE ULTIMATE GUIDE TO THE BRITISH NIGHT OUT

Thank you, Kathryn, Carl, Stasia, Maddie, Corey, Jake, and Dave, for being my experts by experience and for being an integral part of "The Form Book." Your impact on its pages will undoubtedly resonate with readers far and wide, fostering countless unforgettable nights filled with laughter, connection, and sheer joy.

About this Author

Kyle Lightning is an accomplished online content creator turned author. With a passion for writing, Kyle has recently published his first non-fiction book and debut sci-fi romcom novel "Re-connected". Kyle's experiences in the nightlife industry over the past decade have provided him with a wealth of knowledge and insight, which he incorporates into his writing.

Aside from writing, Kyle has also been involved in the film and video industry for over 10 years. He has a YouTube channel with a subscriber base of over 30,000, where he focuses on themes related to mobile technology and social media platforms. Through his channel, Kyle provides valuable insights into how these technologies can be used to enhance daily life.

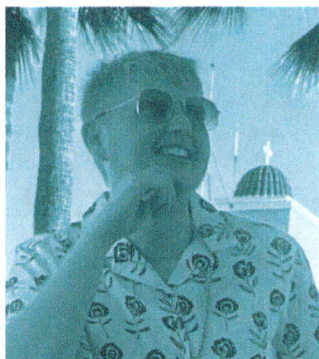

Kyle Lightning is a talented and versatile content creator with a passion for storytelling and a unique perspective on modern relationships and technology.

CONTENTS

The Form Book

SAY HELLO TO GOOD NIGHTS OUT

It can be challenging to plan the perfect night out as they're many individual stages to consider. This book will guide you through each step, from pre-drinks to the after-party, ensuring that you are well-prepared and can make the most of your night out. By breaking down each stage down into the chapters, you will have the tools you need to create a successful night out, no matter what the occasion or location.

The initial section of the book covers how to plan a successful night out, aiming for Good Form by eliminating stress and creating a positive mood. This guarantees that you'll have an unforgettable time and create wonderful memories to reflect on.

The latter part of the book encourages you to reflect on your Form, which should always be a positive experience and shouldn't leave you feeling regret or wanting to never go out again. Breaking down what went wrong on the night through good reflections can change your mindset and help avoid making the same mistakes next time. Bad Form isn't something to dwell on - it's easily rectifiable with the right approach. Besides, everyone has at least one poor night in their lifetime; some worse than others.

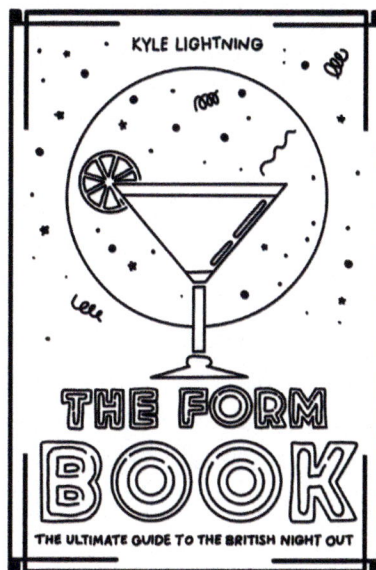

KYLE LIGHTNING

THE FORM BOOK

THE ULTIMATE GUIDE TO THE BRITISH NIGHT OUT

Everything covered in this book has helped to fix either my Form or someone else's, simply by learning to recognise the symptoms of a bad night.

Funnily enough, the picture on the left is where we broke a three-night streak of Bad Form, which is how this book went from a casual conversation with friends to being on store shelves.

What Is Good Form?

Good Form is when you bring out the best version of yourself while socialising with friends- this not only benefits you but also everyone you are with. Good Form is rooted in having a sense of well-being and maintaining a relaxed mindset, enabling you to showcase the optimal version of yourself.

Understanding what your version of Good Form is can help you grow as a person. It can help you become more self-aware, and teach you how to interact with others in a positive and productive way. Good Form can be broken down into two sections - preparation and reflection.

Preparation
The preparation stage is about making decisions and doing activities that promote your health. Looking and feeling great has a massive impact on your day. It's known that being the best version of yourself allows you to get the maximum out of life.

Reflection
The reflection section provides you with the tools to analyze your alcohol consumption and overall state, enabling you to gain insight into what went well and what didn't during your night. By considering both the effects of alcohol and your overall well-being, you can evaluate the outcomes of your choices and actions. This reflection allows you to identify positive aspects that contributed to an enjoyable experience and recognise areas where improvements can be made.

Why Is It Important On A Night Out?
There's no rule book for going out, and there shouldn't be. Going out is all about having fun and making your own traditions, but if you are putting yourself at risk or just waking up full of regret, the Good Form will change your nights for the better.

An example of Good Form for a night out is when you feel like a million pounds in your best clothes, excited to see your friends regardless of rain or shine. The aim is to create this atmosphere every time you go out, not allowing the highs and lows of life to affect the best night of the week.

Having an off night isn't great, but it is nothing to panic about. Everyone will occassionally have a naff night. In most cases, it's forgotten about, and the following night out, you will be back to the standard you expect and enjoy. If the gremlins return on your next night, you may be experiencing a case of Bad Form. It sounds terrible but can be easily rectified with good preparation and a small dose of reflection. Bad Form is quite an easy turnaround.

While you're out you will see some of the most interesting, funny, and crazy things to happen in front of your eyes. Your mood will influence your decisions and reactions.

Enjoying The British Night Out

The night out in Britain is a massive part of British culture. Gathering your friends, dressing up, and going out for a couple of drinks is an iconic thing to do in Britain. From a traditional pub adorned with wooden signs, to a bar boasting vibrant pink neon colours, you'll always find someone indulging in a delightful alcoholic beverage or two.

This book covers all stages of a British night out, from how to do pre-drinks to helping you plan your night out and where to go. It also talks about the importance of wrapping it up correctly.

The British night out can be enjoyed not only by Brits but by anyone around the world. We also take our culture to hot holiday destinations across Europe and other major cities.

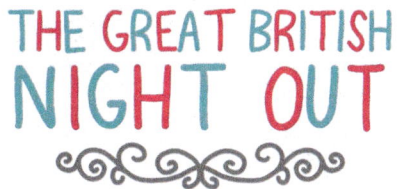

THE GREAT BRITISH
NIGHT OUT

The Form Book

SETTING UP A GOOD FORM

The fate of your night and Form can be decided by the choices that you make before the first sip of the first drink. Treating a night out like a bank heist is good way to have a good time. Get the set up right and the plan will execute flawlessly, allowing you to adapt quickly with your laidback mindset to enjoy the vibes.

Getting a Good Form attitude can start days or even a week before the night. This list of setups can work for most things and not just evenings out with friends. Having a healthy routine and a clear mindset are the two best ingredients for a successful night out.

There are various ways to prepare for a night out. Although not all below will apply to everyone, completing these tasks will have a positive effect on your night.

The list consists of….

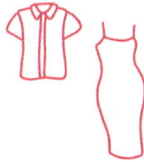

Organised
Outfits

Feeling
Fit

Good Preparation
And Timings

Money To
Burn

Good
Meal

Bring
Fresh

Different
Venues

Feeling Fit

It's tough to match the feeling you get from exercising, the rush of endorphins has a positive effect on how you feel about yourself. The after-workout buzz can be a big boost to your confidence, in both how you feel mentally and how you look physically.

Exercising While Away

When planning a night away from home, it can be beneficial to choose a hotel with a gym if you want to stay on top of your fitness routine. While budget hotels may not offer gym facilities, mid-range and branded hotels usually provide basic equipment such as treadmills, benches, and dumbbell racks. Although the equipment may seem limited, with some creativity, you can still achieve a quality workout that meets your fitness goals. If the hotel does not have a gym, some gym chains allow members to access their facilities in different locations, so you can continue exercising while travelling.

How does being fit generate Good Form?
- Exercising will give you better posture and a more defined muscle tone, which presents you as the best version of yourself.
- People who train together, party together.

Good Meal

Food is so important prior to drinking. The average night out will start and end with food. British culture naturally guides you to the kebab and chip shops after the night has ended.

Setting up the best food Form before the night is vital. Aim for a generous portion of food that fills the plate, this should have the correct balance of food and nutrients you need. Avoid quick snacks, meal deals and chocolate to satisfy your hunger. These are only quick fixes to your hunger and give you a small burst of energy that isn't long-lasting.

Celebration meals and drinks are always tricky to balance. It's highly recommended that you don't drink too much before a meal. The initial euphoria lasts for about 20 minutes, but as time passes, your meal will digest bringing you back to square one. The best practice is to have one drink before you eat and the next with the meal.

The better you prepare your stomach for the tidal wave of booze you are about to consume, the better you'll feel through the next 12 hours.

On the other hand, drinking on an empty stomach is where alcohol basically becomes rocket fuel in your blood, and you will notice the effects of alcohol after one or two drinks. It's a risky game to play. When someone decides to drink on an empty stomach, they should know what they're getting themselves into.

How does eating the right thing generate Good Form?
- Theoretically, the better you eat, the longer you will last before any effects of alcohol start ruining the night.
- You will feel fresher in the morning and have more energy in your reserves, meaning you won't need to force yourself to eat so much. Eating can sometimes be hard if you're not feeling too great.

Being Fresh Before The Night

Feeling good isn't just about the outfits you wear; It takes time to get ready. Doing some self care to your face and hair can make a difference. Sometimes this takes 15 minutes, and occasionally it's a trip to the shops or even a hair appointment. Putting time into how you look really boosts confidence and self-esteem.

Nails

Fresh trim

Apply fragrance

Have a shave

Glamming and Grooming

Skin care

Body hair

Styling your hair

Shower

Lashes

Fresh tan

These are some of the activities that can go on in the glamming and grooming phase. This phase can start two to three days before, and go all the way up to an hour before the night. You might find some get ready to go out while pre-drinking on the night.

The time spent getting ready is like a warm up for your night out. It is where everybody begins to hype each other up and sets the tone for the rest of your time out.

After you have finished getting ready, document it with a few photos. You can use these for dating apps, Instagram or just for you to remember how good you looked.

How does feeling fresh generate Good Form?
- Looking your best is a massive boost to how you feel and see yourself.
- High chance of attracting someone.
- Photo-ready at all times.

Money To Burn

Don't break the bank when you go out, but make sure you're happy with the amount of money you have to go out with; this allows you to enjoy your drinks without being too concerned with the price. Stay in control of your spending and don't give yourself the headache of pending transactions in the morning.

You can have a cost-effective night out by factoring in a few things;

The Location – Cities tend to have more premium bars, which typically have higher-priced drinks. Consider your budget and choose a location accordingly.

Pre-Drinks (Pre's) – British nights out normally start with drinks prior to the evening. You can typically pick up your favourite drink and make it last for the whole of pre's, and it will likely cost half the price of when you're out in the bar/club. If you do pre's perfectly, you can use the drinks when you're out as top-ups rather than of your main source of alcohol.

Additional Costs – Plan for the two ends of the night out. The beginning isn't normally as expensive as the end, and everything from travel to drinks is normally cheaper before 10:30PM. Additional costs to consider within your budget include entry fees to bars and clubs, this can range from £5 to £20.

The average night out costs between £60-£150, but it really depends on the type of drinker you are and where you go out.

How does having money to burn generate Good Form?
- Reduces the stress and allows you to be more present as you are not micro-managing your bank balance.
- When choosing your beverage, you can make your choice based on what you're feeling rather than the cost.
- Your bank balance will be clear of spending-guilt and looming overdrafts.

Organised Outfits

Outfits are an important part of a night out. Wearing something fresh and new is a feeling we all enjoy. Celebration nights are a great reason for a shopping trip or a day out to browse for new clothes and going with friends can build early hype for the night. Everyone loves shopping and getting that next outfit to wear, however, outfits can be expensive, so you don't need to buy a new one every time, even though it's fun to do.

Having a designated section in your wardrobe for nights out and special occasions can be just as important as your holiday clothes. It's important to keep these clothes clean, ironed, and ready to wear, as this gives you more freedom and choice.

When you are travelling away for a night, it's always best to pack 2-3 options, this keeps you covered in case of any spills or wardrobe malfunctions while away. Checking the temperature and weather will influence your choice of outfits. In Spring and Autumn where weather isn't easy to predict, taking a short option and long option will allow for comfort if the weather doesn't go the way it was expected.

AVERAGE TEMPERATURES IN BRITAIN (2022)

JAN 5°c	APR 9°c	JUL 18°c	OCT 13°c
FEB 7°c	MAY 13°c	AUG 18°c	NOV 9°c
MAR 8°c	JUN 15°c	SEP 15°c	DEC 4°c

How does having fresh clothes generate Good Form?

- New clothes will make you feel renewed.
- Keep your 'going out outfits' seperate from your everyday clothing.
- A wardrobe full of clothes ready to go allows you to lend out outfits if one your friends needs a quick fix or comes unprepared.

Different Venues

Spice up your nights by throwing yourself into the unknown with a new experience, even if you come out of a place you haven't visited before with the opinion of "We will never go in there again". The memory of there will give you good laughs for years to come.

Try new venues to keep nights out feeling fresh and like it's the first time you're going out.

Exploring new cities and towns will allow you to discover the area's cultures. You will find strange delicacies and local beverages that will be worth talking about. Look out for interesting shapes and colours of drinks and what they're served in.

Leading your group to a good time is a tough task without experience, as everyone has their own tastes in music and venues. Having lots of experience with the group and knowledge of different clubs, bars and pubs will give you a greater awareness of what is a vibe and what isn't. The ability to make a decision on the venue for everyone is a skill you will learn. It can be hard at first, however it will become subconscious as you master it. We call it the vibe radar and it's the sixth sense for a nightout.

Why does trying new venues generate Good Form?
- New experiences breaks the creature of habit so that you see more.
- Greater awareness of the hotspots increases your chances of being the group leader in new locations.
- New experiences stop nights out becoming stale.

Don't Squeeze Yourself Before The Night

Make sure that you give yourself as much time as possible, so you don't have to rush beforehand, as this can cause stress and dampen the vibes before you go out.

> Everyone's out tonight, are you down?

> I can, but i've just got back home

Spontaneous nights
These can be difficult to do without feeling rushed. Always having an outfit on stand-by will ensure more time to plan for getting ready, food and travel.

> We are all going out tonight, interested?

> I've got a busy one, but I'll squeeze it in

Partying with a busy schedule
Making plans with a busy schedule requires self-control and clear boundaries that protect your existing plans and commitments. How much you drink, and how late you stay are two factors to be aware of when planning to have a great night in a busy period.

> We're all meeting at 21:30, what's your ETA?

> Save me a seat, as I'll get to you for 22:15

Time pressured
Try your best to be transparent with yourself and your friends about your timings. Being clear on where you're realistically going to be, when you say you're going to be there, helps everyone understand what to aim for, and doesn't leave anyone waiting and getting annoyed by being held up.

Preparation

Don't Squeeze Yourself After The Night

Be mindful of your plans the following day and how your night could cause them to be rushed or rearranged. After a night out, you will need recovery time for sleep you lost and energy you used. This time doesn't just mean sleeping in but building yourself back up to feeling 100%.

A good rule of thumb, to help you plan the next day, is to estimate the time you will return home and add 8 hours. This time should be enough time to recuperate.

For example, you return home at 4am - add your 8 hours of rest time and then you should be ready to get going again at around 12pm.

Following this recommendation, by midday you could start any activities or attend any other commitments feeling fresher than you would have if you did not allow rest time!

However, the day after a night out is the perfect excuse for some downtime, either on your own or with the same friends that you went out with. You can recap the night's events and enjoy each other's company without rushing around!

The Morning After

The Form Book

NIGHT PREPARATION

When planning a night out, there are many factors to consider to ensure you have a good time. It could be a quick local night out or an extravagant one where you pack your bags and travel to a city far from home to celebrate your best friend's birthday.

Preparation for a night out requires attention to every small detail, from determining the day of the week to identifying the attendees and deciding on the venue.

You also need to think about the dress code and what you want to wear for the night.

If you're planning a night out away from home, it's important to pack accordingly. The last thing you want is to arrive at your destination and realise you've forgotten something. You will need essentials such as your phone charger and ID, as well as any toiletries you might need.

A night out may follow a similar formula each time, but each experience is unique and different.

Planning the perfect night out can be overwhelming, but this section of the book will guide you through each stage, from deciding on the occasion to choosing the right outfit and coordinating with friends.

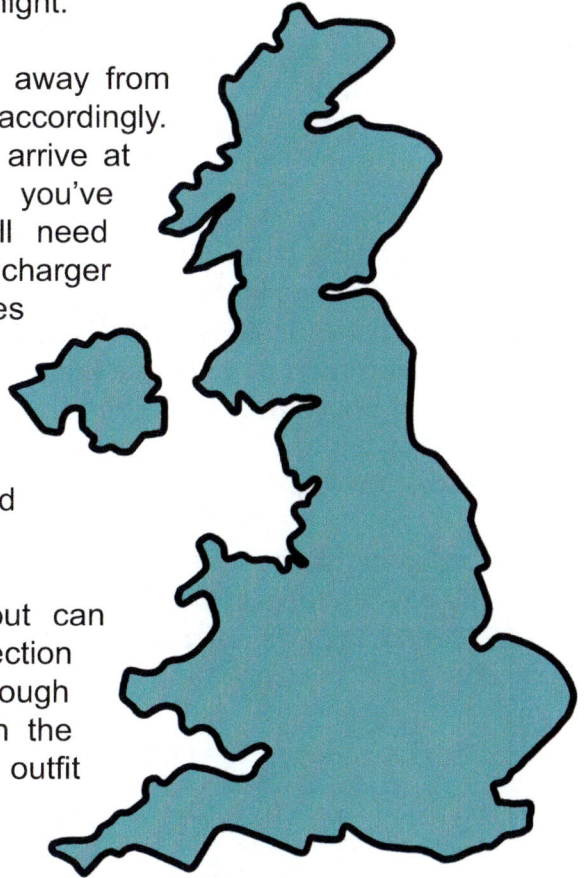

What Day To Go Out?

Friday

The feeling of finishing work on a Friday after a busy week is something we all look forward to, especially when it's followed by a night out. It's common to see work groups out on a Friday as they blow off steam after a long week.

However, Friday nights can feel a bit tight on time if you finish work at 5 pm and want to be out by 8 pm, leaving only three hours to get ready and get to the destination. Good planning and having an outfit prepared allows for a more relaxed time before you head out.

Friday nights out offer the advantage of extending the weekend, allowing for more time to unwind before the start of a new week. Bars and clubs will be bustling with people looking to have a good time.

Saturday

Saturday nights can't come fast enough for many people. Some start their day out early in the afternoon as a lot of people do not work and therefore have more time to enjoy themselves - they can also beat the evening rush this way by finding a good spot to settle into for a while too! Social events, celebrations, and weekend getaways make Saturdays a popular night out. With fewer people also working on Sundays, there's a higher likelihood of a larger turnout.

Saturday nights can last well into Sunday morning, so it's perfectly justifiable to sleep in on Sunday. Taking time to have a meal and dedicating the rest of the day to yourself is an excellent way to recharge for the upcoming week.

Night Out Specials

Bank holidays

Bank holidays are special because they often happen at the perfect time, especially during the spring season. With most bank holidays falling on a Monday, the Sunday leading up to the bank holiday is typically a lively night out, as people have the following day off from work. This makes it the perfect opportunity to enjoy a wild night out with friends. If you tend to avoid going out in the winter due to the cold, these holidays serve as a reminder that warmer evenings are here.

Thursday bank holidays are a rare but exciting occurrence, and they are often some of the best days to party in the UK. These don't count Christmas and New Year. These bank holidays are often linked to the Royal family and can create a mid-week party atmosphere with cities and towns packed with people ready to celebrate. The excitement of a Thursday bank holiday creates a wild Wednesday night, making it the perfect opportunity time to party.

The Three-Night Bender

The bank holiday challenge of going out for three consecutive nights can be a test of both your financial and physical endurance. It's not necessary to drink heavily to participate in the challenge, as the thrill lies in making it out for three nights in a row.

Pay Day Weekend

The feeling of relief when payday arrives and your bank account is replenished can be a great motivator to go out and celebrate. With a full bank balance, it's easier to justify going out.

Both Friday and Saturday night that fall between the 28th-1st of the month is payday weekend for most people and with money in the bank, you will find that everywhere is particularly busy - as people are spending their hard-earned money.

What Type Of Night Is It?

Casual

These nights can be triggered by somebody saying 'Fancy a drink?'. A casual night is normally quickly put together and could go through to last orders, or end an hour after the first drink. It tends to start low-key but with some encouragement, could lead you on to a night of dancing and letting loose.

Prearranged Night

These nights may or may not have a set itinerary, often commencing with pre-drinks or at a familiar location. All those who were invited and expressed their intention to attend will show up unless a major unforeseen circumstance arises. The effort invested In the planning will naturally balance itself out, resulting in a truly enjoyable time.

Group's On Tour

The one or two day mini holiday in a different city or town with your friends, exploring new venues and experiences that aren't accessible near your home. Hotel stays, dining out, and pre-drinks are all part of the adventure. A memorable night in a new location will undoubtedly entice you to plan a return visit.

These thrilling adventures will have you either packed together in one car for a road trip, or whisked away on a train directly to the central station of your destination.

Celebration Night

Birthdays and celebrations are about going the extra mile to make the person who's celebrating have the best night possible. Turning up and buying them a drink is normally all you need to do to make them feel valued and special. Celebration nights can be done anywhere. The night will be pre-planned in most cases and birthdays can also be pre-empted and planned months in advance.

Freshers (Uni Students)

Freshers is typically a night out at a nightclub that is specifically aimed at university students who are new to the area and starting their first year of studies.

Stag/Hen Do's

Stag and hen do's are the final extravagant outing before the momentous day arrives. Stag and hen parties are distinctively tailored to each soon-to-be bride and groom, serving as a celebration of their impending marriage. These gatherings typically cater to a single gender, featuring themed attire and planned activities. It's not uncommon for British stag and hen parties to include naughty games and engaging performers, adding an extra layer of excitement to the festivities.

Stag and hen parties have evolved to include groups venturing into foreign lands, curating unforgettable short breaks abroad. Rather than confining the festivities to a single location, these modern-day celebrations take the party to different countries.

International

When you have a good group of mates who all complement each other and work as a unit, going abroad can be the ultimate memorable experience.

Where To Go?

There's over 1,000 Towns in the United Kingdom with a total of 20,000 areas within those. These will all have at least a pub, a club, or a bar.

Keep your eyes peeled for interesting drinking activities, these may consist of retro arcades, beer pong and mini golf. Novelty experiences like VR Bars, sky restaurants and popular themed venues will appear, but might not be around for long due hype or interest dying out.

Birmingham

Prime Party Location – Broad Street and Brindley Place

Bristol

Prime Party Location – Harbourside and The Traingle

Newcastle

Prime Party Location – Bigg Market, Diamond Strip and Quayside

Manchester

Prime Party Location – Deansgate and Northern Quarter

Liverpool

Prime Party Location – Mathew Street

Sheffield

Prime Party Location – West Street

London

Prime Party Location – It's the Capital

Big Nights Map

Glasgow – Scotland

Prime Party Location – West Regent Street and Union Street

Cardiff – Wales

Prime Party Location – City Centre

Playing At Home Or Away

The Term "Game"

Using the term "Home game" or "Away game" describes what type of night your about to embark on. Football uses this term to informs the fans if the team is playing at the home ground or not. Your home game doesn't typically have to be where you're from, just like football players can change teams.

You're always going to know your home game location better than anywhere else.

Home Game (Most Frequently Visited Night Out)

Your home location is an easier night in most cases, they are also typically cheaper as you're more likely to have a place to stay. Home is classified by your most frequented location for going out, instead of being your hometown. This allows you to frequently go out to the place you enjoy. However, it may be because you have moved town for a fresh start, a job or education. This location would be default choice of going out.

Do expect to bump into friends or people you have met out at this location, also consider that you might know people working in bars who might favour you on doubles or even get you served faster.

If you want to change your home patch for a season or two then keep going to the same town/city routinely.

Away Game

We all love a change of scenery, whether you've been to the location before or it's the first time. These trips can sometimes feel like a mini holiday. These nights out mostly consist of packing a small suitcase or bag. You will take the bare essentials with you.

Packing And Hotel Stay

- ☐ SLEEPWEAR / LOUNGEWEAR
- ☐ SOCKS & UNDERWEAR
- ☐ DRINK OF CHOICE
- ☐ BEST OUTFIT
- ☐ BACK UP OUTFIT
- ☐ TOILETRIES
- ☐ PHONE CHARGER
- ☐ TRAVEL SPEAKER
- ☐ ID
- ☐ MEDICINES

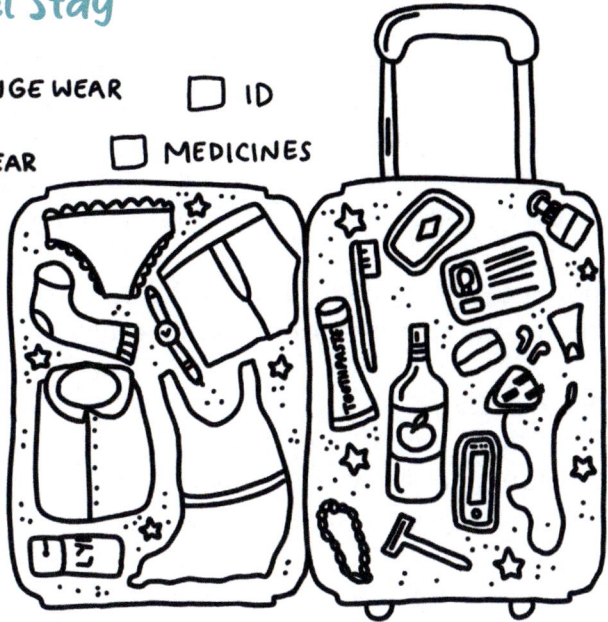

Being in a different city makes time feel faster. An hour can fly by, feeling more like just 20 minutes. The excitement of new sights, sounds, and experiences keeps you engaged, and before you know it, time slips away. Allow yourself more time than you think when planning to meet up or get ready.

Allocating additional time in your schedule helps mitigate stress and ensures smooth handling of unexpected delays.

Hotel stays are always fun as your room becomes your hub for the night. In Britain, you can play a good game of hotel room roulette, which could have you reserving the oldest hotel room in the city centre, or you could fall lucky with a smart tv, modern interior and a room that feels like a penthouse suite. Some hotels also have breakfast included with the room which adds value to your stay.

Whether you do pre's or not, you can enjoy an away game in every season of the year. Each city you visit has its own secrets, culture and weird drinks to discover.

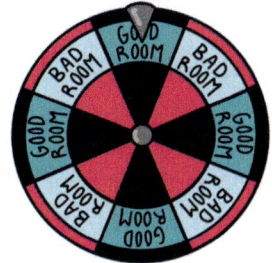

What To Wear?

Nightlife is the best place to dress to impress, even if you want to impress yourself. Putting on the best/newest clothes is such a rewarding feeling. There aren't always rules on what to wear, although some venues have certain dress codes. Joggers and casual/sports trainers may get you refused entry to some bars and clubs.

When it comes to picking your style, make sure you know the dress code so you can plan appropriate outfits.

Casual Night

This attire would be normal and acceptable everywhere and at all times of the year. Going out for a few intended drinks which might turn into a full-blown night out wouldn't be bad in casual clothes. This is an outfit that would be very adaptable in many situations.

Best Outfits

You must mean business (and not in the 9-5 way.) These outfits make you feel like a million pounds. It may take two or three outfits before you find the one that you will wear, add a quick spray of your best scent to complete the outfit. Most photos taken of you in these clothes would be profile picture material. Your favourite brands and luxurious items would fall into this category.

The term "Out Out" is used to tell someone your intentions for your evening plans. Typically dressed up and out for more than one drink. Short and long-sleeved shirts, skinny jeans, cocktail dresses, and fancy blazers are just some of the many types of clothing that are specifically marketed for going out out.

Formal Attire

Going out for a couple of drinks in formal clothes isn't appropriate. Formal attire, such as suits and evening dresses, are typically worn at formal occasions such as weddings, funerals, interviews, and proms.

Examples of occasions where you might see people dressed in formal attire on a night out could include an after-party following a formal work event or a wedding reception.

Fancy Dress

These nights don't appear out of nowhere, so there's plenty of time to plan your outfit. Themed parties and Halloween are the most recognisable nights for funny and interesting costumes. If you struggle to be creative with your choice of attire, there are two options for you to try and help inspire you.

The first option is to browse online for ideas or browse online stores for costumes; filtering by the most popular will show you what others have brought from that site.

The other option is most high streets have a party/costume shop which will have plenty of options to help choose a simple or expensive outfit. If that fails, you could ask the person manning the shop.

Dressing up in a fancy costume is all about having fun, so don't be afraid to join in the festivities even if you feel silly at first. Remember, everyone else is dressed up and having a good time, and they'll appreciate you joining in on the fun.

The Form Book

PRE-DRINKS

Pre-drinks are a part of British night culture, typically held in a home or student residence. It's a chance to gather everyone together before the night kicks off, not only to warm up the vibe for the evening, but also to ensure that everyone is in the same place and ready to head to the next destination without having to wait around for stragglers.

Every pre-drinks session is unique to each household, with some using it as a mini party complete with dancing and music, while others take the opportunity to have a drink and get ready for the night ahead.

To help get the party started, choose your drink and your favourite party song. Ask your smart speaker or streaming service to create a personalised playlist to party along to.

Playing classic drinking games or social games can be a fun way to break the ice and get to know each other at pre-drinks. Whether it's a game of cards or something more daring, these activities can help create a relaxed and enjoyable atmosphere for everyone. For students and friends new to the group, pre-drinks can be a great way to get to know each other and form closer bonds. The more memorable the night, the more likely everyone will be looking forward to the next pre-drinks with you.

PRE'S STREET

Pre's Playlist Starters

Heaven - DJ Sammy 2001 Club

Gecko – Becky Hill & 2014 Future house

The Key, The Secret - Urban Cookie Collective 1993 Pop

Ayo – Chris Brown & Tyga 2015 Hip-Hop

Tokyo – Dwin 2020 Dance/Electronic

Set you free – N-Trance 1995 Club

Don't stop believing - Journey 1981 Rock

Juliet and Romeo - Martin Solveig 2019 Dance

Head & Heart - Joel Corry x MNEK 2021 Dance

Timber – Pitbull 2013 Pop

Good Vibes – HRVY 2020 Pop

Insomnia – Faithless 1990 House

Choose Your Pre-Drink

 # MENU

On Tap

Grab some cans of your favourite alcoholic beverage.

Beers - Have a few cold ones with a pack of bottled beers.

Cider - Serve your cider with a glass with ice.

Lager - Sip on the iconic light and fresh taste of lager.

Cocktails

Get creative with fruit juice by making your own cocktails.

Pick up some pre-made mixers from the supermarket.

Use your biggest jug to make a cocktail pitcher.

Keep It Classy

Keep it classy by sharing a bottle of red or white wine.

Bring a bottle of bubbly to pop with your friends.

Club Classics

VK - Bring a box of random flavours.

Smirnoff Ice - Adult lemonade with a boozy citrus twist.

Spirits

Vodka - Ignite the night with the clear rocket fuel!

Rum - Discover the soul of the caribbean.

Malibu - Dive into the coconut oasis and taste pure summer.

Whiskey - Surrender to the gentle embrace of whiskey's warmth.

Gin - Crafted to be the perfect partner for tonic.

Soft Drinks

Fizzy Pop

Fresh Juice

Energy Drink

Verbal Games

House Rules

Set interesting rules that your friends aren't allowed to break. For example, you can require everyone to drink with their non-dominant hand only, prohibit swearing, disallow the use of anyone's name during the game, or require players to refrain from checking their phones. Make sure everyone knows what the forfeit is for breaking any of these rules - the forfeit can be anything you want it to be. These rules will challenge your friends and make the game more exciting!

Parking Rules

To add an element of fun to your drinking session with friends, you can play the role of the annoying parking attendant. Keep an eye on everyone's glasses and call out anyone whose glass is too close to the edge. To measure the distance from the edge of the table to the glass, use your index finger and push it against the rim until your knuckle touches the table. If you manage to push their glass even slightly on the table, they must drink three fingers worth of their drink as a penalty.

Shot Clock

The point of this game is to take a shot every time the alarm goes off. As a group, choose how long the timer lasts; The duration is best decided on the night as it depends how long you've got until you are going out and you want to get at least a couple of shots in. Keep it random (e.g. 47 minutes).

Adding a forfeit to the challenge can spice up the game, for example changing social media bios, profile pictures, and statuses can act as a deterrent from giving up.

Social Games

Never Have I Ever

This game is a popular party game where players take turns making statements beginning with the phrase "Never have I ever." These statements usually describe something that a player has never done before, such as "Never have I ever pulled a sick day after a night out" or "Never have I ever lied to my parents."

If a player has done the activity described in the statement, they have to take a drink. If they haven't done it, they don't do anything. The game can be played with any number of players, and the statements can range from silly and lighthearted to more serious or personal.

"Never have I ever" is a popular icebreaker game that is often played at parties or social gatherings. It's a fun way for people to get to know each other better and share their experiences, especially if they don't know each other well.

Secret Operations

For an entertaining challenge during your night out with friends, set a mission to complete by morning. Choose a habit you typically engage in while you're out and challenge yourself to not do it. Every member of the group has their own mission to complete.

For example, if you are known for taking too many photos while out with friends, challenge yourself to limit your photography to five shots per night.

If you succeed, celebrate your accomplishment in the morning.

Seven Seconds

Challenge your friends to list 3 things, within 7 seconds, in a random category that you give them. For example, 'Name 3 party holiday destinations'. If they successfully give you 3 destinations , then they pass the challenge, but if they fail, they must do the forfeit. Again, this forfeit can be anything you want it to be.

Jackbox.tv

Over the last decade, there has been a noticeable increase in the popularity of digital games as a form of entertainment in the party scene. This trend can be attributed to the convenience and accessibility of digital games, as they are often easy to set up and don't require downloads for guests to participate.

Jackbox.tv is a highly popular digital game platform that offers a unique and interactive gaming experience. Unlike traditional console games, Jackbox.tv utilises a device with a web browser as the primary means of playing. This makes it extremely accessible, as players can easily join in on the fun using their own smartphones, tablets, or laptops.

The games available on Jackbox.tv are known for their randomness and unpredictable nature, with many quiz-style games featuring questions that are often absurd or nonsensical. This adds an element of humor to the gameplay, as players are encouraged to provide humorous or ridiculous answers in response.

One of the main advantages of Jackbox.tv is its ease of setup and accessibility for guests. Jackbox.tv only requires the host to have a PC or game console with a copy of one of the games, as well as a wifi connection.

For guests to join in, all they need to do is navigate to the Jackbox.tv website and enter the room pin that appears on the host's TV screen. This streamlined process allows for quick and easy setup, making it an ideal choice for party entertainment or group gatherings.

Traditional Pack Of Cards

A deck of cards is often considered a good addition to a party because it provides a variety of games and activities that can be played with a group of people. Many classic card games such as Poker, Blackjack, Chase the Ace and Rummy are popular and can be turned into drinking games.

A pack of cards are inexpensive and widely available, with decks ranging from basic to humorously themed.

Decks of cards are highly sought after by university students, to the extent that some universities even provide them to prospective students during open days.

Poker

To play Poker, players make bets based on the perceived value of their hand compared to the other players. The goal is to have the highest-ranking hand at the end of the game, or to bluff others into believing that you do.

Black Jack

To play Blackjack, players aim to get a hand value of 21 or as close to it as possible without going over. The dealer deals two cards to each player and to themselves, with one card face up and the other face down. The player can then choose to hit (take another card) or stand (keep their current hand) in an attempt to beat the dealer's hand.

Chase The Ace

To play Chase the Ace, remove one ace from the deck and deal the remaining cards equally among all players without revealing them. Players take turns picking a card from the player on their right and aim to form pairs of the same numbers. The game continues until one player is left with the remaining ace, and that player is declared the loser.

Kings Cup

One of the most renowned drinking games of all time. It's popularity comes from the simplicity and ease to set up. The game is exciting, but full of risk. All you need for this game is a pack of cards and a glass of any size. Each card determines an action and you continue until someone breaks the circle of cards around the glass. They must then drink the king's cup, which will be a mix of other players drinks.

To set-up the game, place your glass down in the centre of everybody, and place all the cards face down in a circle around the glass with no breaks in the circle.

The page to the right displays the common actions for each card, but you can modify them to your liking.

Alternative cards rules from other versions
J – Never Have I Ever
5 – Bust a jive (dancing competition)
5 – Five Guys (boys) 6 – Chicks (girls)
8 – Date (pick a date for the Night)
King – Social (everyone drinks instead of filling a cup)

Kings Cup Rules

A — Waterfall, **everyone drinks simultaneously** and can only stop when the person to their right does. The initiator is the first to stop.

2 — The power of two, you have the power to **choose who drinks.**

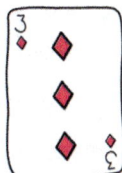

3 — Three is me, **you drink.**

4 — Fours are whores, **girls drink.**

5 — **Thumb Master,** the designated player can place their thumb on the table and everyone else must follow suit. The last person drinks.

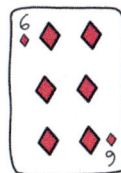

6 — Six is dicks, **boys drink.**

7 — Seven is heaven. **Raise your finger** anytime and the last person to do so drinks. Stay alert to avoid being the one to drink.

8 — Eight is your mate, **pick someone to drink with.**

9 — Nine is a **rhyme**, pick a word and take turns around the group rhyming that word, and the one who pauses or hesitates must drink.

10 — **Pick a category** like "Clothes shops" and have everyone take turns naming one. If someone can't think of a new one, they drink.

J — You're the judge, **make a rule**, if a player breaks the rule, they must take a drink. this rule will only be in effect until the next Jack card is played.

Q — Question master, **ask questions** to anyone and if anybody answers your question, they must drink.

K — Kings cup, **pour your drink into a communal cup** to make the king's concoction. Players usually fill the cup one-fourth full.

The Form Book

THE ADVENTURE BEGINS

When you step outside for the first time on a night out, that's when the real action begins. If you've been pre-drinking beforehand, you're likely to be pumped up and ready to go. Just remember that a night out can be like a battlefield - you never know what you'll encounter or what you might end up doing.

This section will break down the different types of venues and offer advice on how to approach them to fit your night. Pubs, bars, and clubs all have their own unique characteristics and require different game plans.

Pubs are generally more laid-back and ideal for casual drinks and conversations with friends.

Bars tend to be more focused on cocktails and often have a livelier atmosphere.

Clubs are all about the music and dancing.

By understanding the different vibes and expectations of each venue, you can plan your night accordingly and maximise your fun.

If you're planning to go out early, around 7pm, then clubs may be off the cards as they are closed until later, and don't start getting busy until 11:30. In this case, pubs and bars are your options, pubs are a great place to start your night as they usually offer a more casual and social atmosphere. You can catch up with your friends, have a pint, and maybe even grab a bite to eat before moving on to the next venue.

In smaller towns, there may be certain plans you do more than once due to limited variety of venues, while in larger cities, the options may be more vast and allow for more spontaneity. It's always good to have an idea of what you want from the night and plan accordingly,

Sometimes the best nights happen when you go with the flow and see where the night takes you. Keep in mind that every night out is unique and will differ in their own ways.

Where To Party?

Pub

Whether old or modern, pubs are always welcoming, most offer a wide variety of hot food and cool refreshing drinks. Some venues even feature live sports or interactive pub quizzes for added entertainment. Pubs are a great meeting spot and can keep the good times rolling late into the night.

(Prime hours 2pm-10pm)

Bar

Fancy drinks, neon signs, and attractive designs - bars are where you can enjoy bright-coloured cocktails and socialise with friends. Bars often serve food and play music, making it the perfect in-between option for those looking for something between a pub and a club. Some bars will have guest DJs that turn the place into a small pop-up club.

(Prime hours 4pm-12am)

Club

Having a vibrant and energetic atmosphere is what a club is all about, with dynamic lighting and music-themed rooms to dance in. Dress codes often apply to maintain a level of elegance. Entry fees, VIP tables, and appearances from special guests and popular DJs make the venue a must-visit. Clubs are for all-night partying that can often go on until sunrise.

(Prime hours 10:30pm-4am)

Game Plan

Make sure to plan your night's destinations in advance. This will influence everyone's style and what they drink through the night. Here's a few popular plans:

Pre's → Club

Pre's → Bar → Club

Bar → Bar → Club

Bar → Club

Pre's → Bar → Bar

Bar → Bar

Club → Club

Pre's → Pub → Bar → Club (All-rounder)

Pub → Pub → Bar → Bar → Club → Club (The Double Down)

Pub Crawl

Bar Crawl

Hen do/Stag do

Day Drinking

Benefits Of Pres And Pubs

Pre-Drinks

Pre-drinks are a popular way to save money in the early stage of the night, while also a being great way to socialise with your friends before going out. The option to pick your own music and play games can allow everyone to get more hyped for the night.

Pros
+ Provides a chance to play drinking games and break the ice with new friends.
+ Cheapest start to the night.
+ Allows everyone to arrive when they can.
+ A space to potentially get changed while pre-drinking.

Cons
- Requires someone to have a suitable private residence.
- The host has to tidy up after.
- Possibility of running out of alcohol and mixers, with no way of restocking easily.

The Pub

Going to the pub on a night out is a great option because it offers a laid-back and relaxed atmosphere; Perfect for catching up with friends or meeting new people. With a wide variety of beers, ales, and ciders on tap. Pub menus often feature traditional comfort food and classic pub dishes.

Pros
+ Offers a wide variety of alcoholic and non-alcoholic drinks.
+ Usually has a good selection of food.
+ Provides a space to engage in catch ups and deep conversations with friends.
+ Indoor wood burners for cozy winter nights and outdoor beer gardens for a cold drink in the summer.

Cons
- Difficulty finding a seat or table especially during peak hours.
- Closes the earliest out of the venues in most cases.
- Limited or outdated entertainment options.
- Can be a 'Cliquey' atmosphere.

Benefits Of Bars And Clubs

The Bar

This establishment serves alcoholic beverages, along with non-alcoholic drinks. It's a popular social gathering place where people come to relax, socialise, and have a good time. Bars often have a specific theme or decor that sets the tone for the experience.

Pros
+ Wide range of cocktails and mocktails.
+ Often have a happy hour or drink specials.
+ Bar staff are entertaining and friendly.
+ Music is usually not as loud as it is in clubs.
+ Good place to meet new people.

Cons
- Limited food menu.
- Highest cost per hour out of the venues.
- Longer waiting times to be served.
- Fewer tables, which might require booking in advance.

The Club

Clubs are a vibe, they're know typically to have a dress code to ensure a certain level of presentation and atmosphere. The atmosphere is electric with the potential for exclusive DJs and special guests to arrive on certain nights.

Pros
+ They are often open late which makes them easier to plan around.
+ Often feature popular DJs and live music performances.
+ Multiple music genres in different themed rooms.
+ Great way to meet new people.
+ The music, lighting and visuals at the club create a unique atmosphere.

Cons
- Cost of entry.
- Increased risk of assault and harassment.
- The high volume of music can make it difficult to socialise.
- Incidents of alcohol and drug abuse among individuals.

The Night Out Know-Hows

Journey Juice

You will buy this drink between two venues. Typically, this is when you're about to walk for 10-20-minutes to another venue. A prime example would be if you were travelling from the city centre to a location just outside the main venues and attractions.

Off-licences and convenience stores are brilliant for buying some journey juice. Not only will you find alcoholic drinks that you have never even heard of, but flavours you wouldn't even think of putting together. The price of a drink is usually cheap and sold separately, avoiding wasted cans and money.

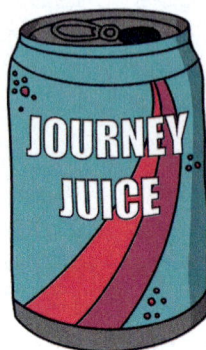

Breaking The Seal

Don't break the seal or you will be receiving fast track tickets to the loo. As they say, breaking the seal is when you first use the toliet after drinking alcohol, which can lead to a seemingly endless cycle of bathroom breaks.

Taking Your Photos

Photos on a night out can be a great way to capture memories and remember the fun times you had with your friends. Whether you prefer portrait or landscape orientation.

If you want a good photo of yourself, choose portrait orientation to capture the best composition of you and your outfit.

If you want to capture photos of the group, the atmosphere and surroundings of the night out, then landscape would be a better choice.

Taking photos has become so fast and convenient that you can easily switch between portrait and landscape orientations.

Bypassing Online Dating

Meeting a potential love interest while out and about can be an exciting and unexpected way to find a connection with someone. Even if you weren't necessarily looking for someone, you never know who you might stumble across and hit it off with. While the party atmosphere and loud music can make it difficult to have meaningful conversations, there is something to be said for the natural attraction that can arise in these settings. When you're out, you tend to look and feel your best, and the same goes for those around you.

If you happen to make a connection with someone while out, it's important to capitalise on the moment and exchange contact information before parting ways. You never know if you'll see them again, so it's crucial to get their phone number or social media handle.

The One Night Stand

The one night stand typically occurs when two people meet each other and feel sexually attracted to one another. They engage in a sexual encounter, usually without any prior emotional connection or commitment to each other. Some people go out specifically looking for one night stands.

02:30 Myth

If you are unaware of the significance of 2:30 am, it is believed that nothing interesting or noteworthy happens after that time. The chances of successfully meeting or picking up someone after 2:30 is drastically reduced, almost as if the odds are stacked against you.

It's important to recognise that if the atmosphere has been dull and uninspiring for the previous hour or two, it's highly unlikely that things will suddenly pick up in the last hour. In fact, the opposite is often true, as the energy and excitement of the evening may have already dissipated, you may be better to call it a night and head out for a nice meal instead. Sometimes, it's best to accept that the night has run its course, than waste any more time and money than you need too.

The Form Book

EXTRA TIME

When you step out of the club with your mates, it often feels like the end of the night. This moment can be compared to the last scene in a movie - It won't be the most exciting part, but it will tie up any loose ends.

As you step away from the last venues doors, you enter the transition phase. Within the next hour, you'll most likely find yourself back home, but during that time, there are opportunities to make the most of the moment. You might decide to stop by a late-night food joint with your friends, satisfying those post-night-out cravings. Alternatively, you might opt to call a taxi, joining your friends in a jovial conversation during the ride, reliving the highlights of the night and sharing laughter over inside jokes. These brief yet precious moments, filled with good food and cherished camaraderie, add the perfect touch to conclude the night's adventures.

The next stage of the book covers prep before you head to bed and how to keep yourself and others safe when drinking. Although most is common sense, it is important to take thee steps to ensure that you are able to have a good time and minimise the chances of suffering the consequences of excessive alcohol consumption and making yourself unwell.

Refueling Before Going Home

Late Night Meal

Partying out late at night uses a lot of energy and can leave you hungry in the morning, this is when your stomach becomes empty and delicate. Eating a heavy meal before going to sleep can help to sober you up a little bit and prevent bad hangovers in the morning.

It's common to come across a row of fast-food restaurants that typically remain open after midnight. While the food they serve may not be the healthiest, it can actually be better for you than you think.

Indulge in a delightful array of options including beef burgers, chicken nuggets, and even pizzas, while relishing your meal from the comfort of a table adorned with the most uncomfortably charming chairs, all served in a lovely polystyrene container.

Water

Before calling it a night, opt for a refreshing glass of water. This simple step won't cost you anything, but it can make a big difference in the morning. Revitalising your body with proper hydration after consuming alcohol and engaging in a night filled with dancing and walking will result in a heightened sense of refreshment and alertness the following day. By replenishing lost fluids, you can counteract the dehydrating effects of alcohol.

"The great thirst" is a common experience among those who have consumed alcohol. As the body tries to process and eliminate the alcohol, it can cause dehydration, leading to a feeling of extreme thirst. This can occur in the early morning, and often leads to consuming large quantities of water in an attempt to alleviate the sensation.

Better mornings all start by filling up your glass and bringing it with you to bed.

Close Your Night

Home Safe Checks

Home Safe Checks are a simple but important step to take after a night out with friends. It's always a good idea to check in with your group, even if you only saw them 30 minutes ago. Letting each other know that you've made it home safely can prevent unnecessary worry and help ensure everyone stays in the loop. It's easy for things to go wrong, and 10 minutes can turn into 3 hours or more if someone gets lost or falls.

Avoid The Oven

It's important to avoid making your own food on the hob or oven when you have had a few drinks. It may seem unlikely, but there's a high chance that you could fall asleep while the food is preparing.

A friend of mine once put a frozen pizza in the oven and fell asleep on his bed, only to come back to a burnt carcass. In an attempt to redeem themselves, they put another pizza in the oven and sat on the sofa to avoid falling asleep, only to fall asleep once again and be woken up by the sound of the fire alarm.

Lying On Your Side

Lying on your back after a night out can be quite dangerous, so it's important to avoid this position and instead lie on your side to reduce the risk of choking in case you're sick in your sleep and this allows for easier breathing.

If your friend has had too much to drink and can't seem to find their way to the bed, don't be afraid to tell them to sleep on their side. And if they're stubborn, just turn them over yourself. It's the responsible thing to do. Friends don't let friends sleep on their backs like overturned turtles.

It's important to look out for your friends and make sure they're sleeping in a safe position.

The Form Book

REFLECTIONS

This section of the book helps deconstruct every aspect of a night out and provides a comprehensive analysis of behaviours, helping you to identify a potential moment that could be questionable or a bad decision that may influence your Form.

We created these measures to allow you to discuss your night's highs and lows easily. This method has been our lifeline to open up conversations about Bad Form. Asking your friends for their thoughts on your performance from the previous night is an excellent way to remember and reminisce about the events that took place.

Reflecting on your experiences has always been beneficial, learning to look back and learning from any mistakes is a great way to grow as a person. Our first reflection involves evaluating your alcohol intake and determining where you are on the scale from sober to completely wasted.

Our second reflection connects to the Good Form cue cards, which consist of the essential elements of most nights out. This concise list of items served as the inspiration for this book, allowing readers to reflect and chuckle over the mishaps and highlights of their experiences.

The two scales presented in the book utilise a colour-coded system to help categorise the information provided. The pages provide a comprehensive breakdown of all the details. The goal is to aim for anything in the green zones, which represents a good night out.

1,2,3 Scale - Blue - Green - Pink

Form Breakdown - Green - Orange - Red

This tool is designed to improve your night out experiences and aid in understanding whether you have pushed yourself too hard. It is not meant to be used by friends to intentionally degrade you based on this information. Remember to use it as a positive tool for personal growth and reflection.

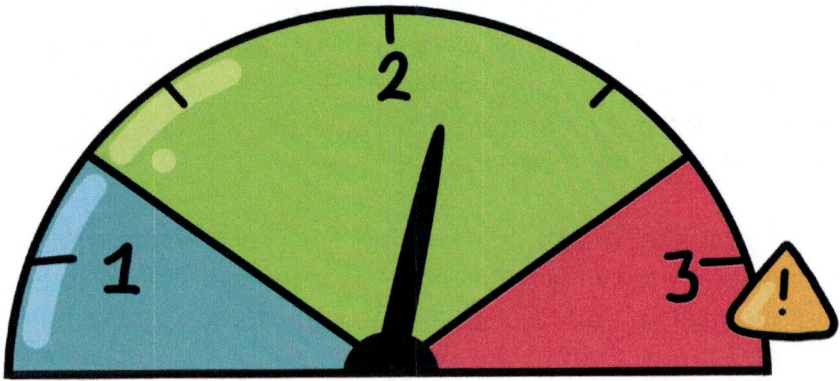

The 1 2 3 Scale

Here's how to visualise alcohol consumption easily, using three stages which are based on the amount of alcohol consumed. This approach is useful for understanding your limits, as everyone's alcohol tolerance varies.

Stages one and two represent levels of good alcohol control, where you are still within your limits. However, once you reach stage three, you have exceeded your limit, and this can lead to negative consequences such as being sick or putting yourself in a dangerous situation.

Therefore, it's crucial to be mindful of how much you are drinking and to recognise when you have reached your limit. Understanding your limit will ensure a safe and enjoyable night out.

Being able to recognise when your friends are moving towards stage three is a valuable skill. This skill enables you to prevent your friends from putting themselves in danger or causing distress to themselves or others.

Stage One

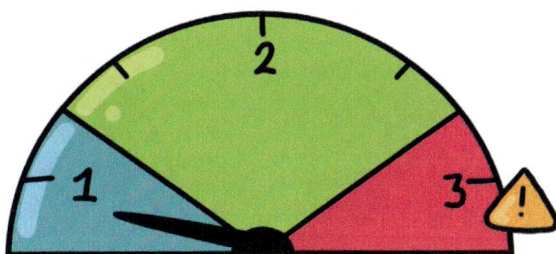

The **blue zone** signifies the beginning phase, where you can enjoy a few drinks with your mates, but also continue your day if you wanted too. Taking a single sip of alcohol immediately places you in the blue zone, and whether you decide to continue with more drinks is entirely your choice.

Engaging in social activities with friends while having a drink can have positive effects on our well-being, Stage one will offer the ability to carry out daily tasks without being affected by the alcohol buzz and avoiding distractions or silliness.

As appealing as stage one is, it's important to recognize that it's only a small window of operation. This means that as soon as you start feeling the effects of alcohol, you essentially cross the border into stage two.

One of the drawbacks to stage one is that if you've spent the last couple of hours getting ready to enjoy a few hours of socialising and drinking, it can be disappointing to arrive and find out that the night is over after just one drink. Back in 2015, the term "session" was all the rage, and if you were going out for a session, you were definitely aiming for stage two. In other words, you were ready to let loose and have a good time. So, if you're looking for a wild night, You might find you're out for more than a few.

It's crucial to remember that even if you don't feel the effects of alcohol after one or two drinks, drinking and driving should never be an option. Driving under the influence of alcohol is illegal and incredibly dangerous.

Stage Two

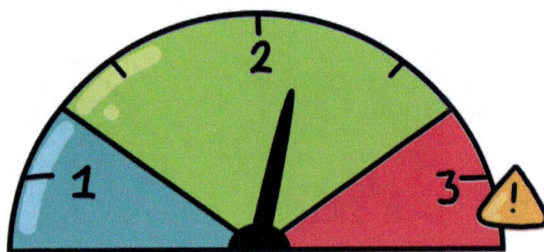

Stage 2, known as the **optimal drinking zone**, is where you ideally want to be when you're out with your friends. It represents a safe alcohol level that typically results in minimal or mild hangovers. In the diagram, the range is larger because this is where the majority of your night will be spent. It's designed to demonstrate that even the tiniest amount of alcohol can lead to a satisfying and enjoyable night out.

Knowing your limits and being aware of what you can handle is crucial for ensuring a good night and a productive day afterwards. It's admirable to be the person who can enjoy a night of partying and wake up the next day feeling energised and ready to take on any challenges that come your way.

Even as you approach the upper end of the green section, you can still experience the same minimum morning-after effects as when you first entered stage two. There are generally no significant drawbacks to being in stage two of alcohol consumption. However, it's essential to remain vigilant and pay attention to any signs that you may be getting closer to stage three. You know your body best, so if you sense that you might be becoming more intoxicated, take proactive measures to prevent the needle from progressing into the next section. This can be done by reducing your alcohol intake, or stopping entirely and switching to water.

Stage Three

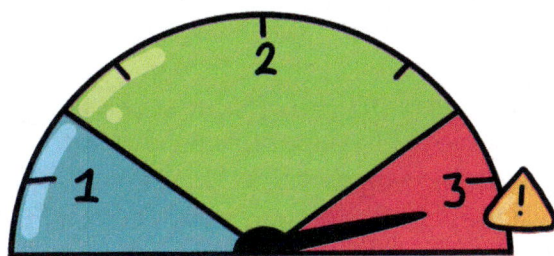

It's important to remember that everyone has their limits when it comes to drinking alcohol, it is very common to reach the third stage at least once in your lifetime. However, if you find yourself getting too drunk while you're out, it's not too late to take action and reduce the likelihood of experiencing any of the unpleasant signs associated with stage three.

On The Night
- Memory loss
- Blackouts
- Sickness
- Being uncomfortably hot
- Falls/can't stand
- Sleeping/unconscious.

The Morning After
- Anxious mornings/regret
- Not being able to function
- Hot and uncomfortable
- Wishy-washy stomach
- Next day sickness
- Severe hangover
- Cuts and bruises (from falling)
- Concussion (from falling)

The effects of **stage 3** are the result of having consumed a toxic amount of alcohol. While stages 1 and 2 can be enjoyable experiences, it's important to avoid stage 3 as it can leave you vulnerable and in danger on a night out. One of the biggest risks of being so drunk is finding yourself alone and unable to function properly. In fact, many people's horror stories from a night out stem from being in stage 3.

It's important to avoid making a mess of yourself and to look out for your friends. If you notice your friends venturing towards stage 3, make sure to bring them back around straight away. This will avoid any dramas that can write-off the current night or into the next day.

Positive Form

Positive Form - The primary objective of a night out is to have an enjoyable experience. The focus is on relaxing, letting go, and enjoying oneself, which is what attracts many individuals to participate in such activities. Ultimately, the goal is to have a good time and create positive memories.

Confidence – Confidence is key. Going out with minimal anxieties allows you to relax, chill and blow off some steam which is one key factor to feeling great after a night out.

Dance – You don't have to be a dancer to score high in this category. Hitting the dance floor can still be a great way to have fun and let loose while you're out. Don't be afraid to get out there and move to the music! If you can let loose and have fun without constantly needing a drink, that shows great Form.

Sociability – A night out with friends doesn't necessarily mean you won't interact with others. Social interactions are inevitable. It's a great opportunity to make new contacts and expand your social circle, which is one of the best things about going out.

Chat – Having a good chat helps in all areas on a night out, whether it's striking up a conversation with new people, being a wingman for your best mate, or chatting up someone you find attractive. Not only does it create a positive and friendly atmosphere, but it also helps to build connections and foster relationships. So don't be afraid to put yourself out there.

Drinks – Finding the perfect balance between having a great time and consuming just the right amount of alcohol is decisive for a successful night out. It's essential to pace yourself and listen to your body.

Team player – Being a team player on a night out means being there for your friends and making sure they are safe, whether it's by ensuring they are okay or intervening to prevent them from drinking excessively and getting into fights or other sticky regretful situations.

Being a team player often happens subconsciously. However, it's important to take action when needed. A significant aspect of being a team player involves diffusing or avoiding difficult situations. The ability to remain calm and composed is essential to being an effective team member. By keeping a level head and defusing potentially volatile situations.

Problem solver - Dealing with unexpected issues on a night out is strangely common, and sometimes you may find yourself helping a stranger in need. From lost phones to broken heels, the list of weird side quests you can end up assisting with is endless. However, taking the time to show compassion for others around you, even when it means sacrificing some of your own enjoyment, truly demonstrates your character. It's a reminder that sometimes the best moments on a night out come from helping others.

Being the wingman - Typically refers to a person who supports and assists their friend or colleague in social situations, particularly in dating scenarios. The wingman's role is to provide social reinforcement, help break the ice, and create a more comfortable atmosphere for their friend. This can involve engaging in conversation, making introductions, and offering encouragement and support.

Having an blast - Knowing that a night out was truly enjoyable and worthwhile can be a great mood booster the next day. It can make it easier to face the challenges ahead, and the positive memories can stay with you for a long time.

Questionable Form

Questionable Form - refers to actions that could either have a positive or unknown effect, and while not necessarily serious problems, they are things that could have been avoided with better judgment.

Drunk calls and texts – Alcohol can give you the liquid courage to make that late-night call or send that risky text, but beware: what seems like a great idea at the time may not be so great in the sober light of day. And trust us, those texts will definitely come back to haunt you in the morning.

Let's hope the text is in your favour when you wake up the next morning.

Don't text the ex – Don't break the golden rule of texting the ex unless you want to feel like you're starring in your own romantic comedy, go ahead and text the ex. But just remember, the morning after might feel more like a horror movie. So, unless you're looking to be chased down by an angry mob with pitchforks, maybe avoid that one.

No matter how good the breakup was, your ex is your ex for a reason, so why ruin your night by texting them? It's time to let loose and have some fun!

Purchases – Sometimes when the night is a bit lacklustre, you find yourself scrolling on your phone and stumble upon a purchase you've been eyeing for a while, or convince yourself that you suddenly need something you never knew existed before.

Waking up to a bank account that's taken a hit or a package you don't remember ordering can be a surprise, thanks to the late-night online shopping spree fuelled by boredom and alcohol. It's like Christmas came early, but with a twist.

Spilling a drink - It can happen to the best of us - it's not just the liquid that's being wasted, it's also the money you spent on it! Whether it's due to overexcitement on the dance floor or simply being a bit tipsy, it's never a good feeling to see your drink go flying. And if you spill someone else's drink, it can be even worse - you might end up buying them a new one.

Let's hope that your outfit hasn't become a victim of the drink spillage as well.

Chatting rubbish - When under the influence, our inhibitions loosen, and we find ourselves capable of uttering silly remarks. Though innocuous, these statements may not always make sense. When asked to explain, one might simply respond with a shrug and say, "I don't know mate, I was pissed."

> **Respect The Group -** It's important to be mindful of everyone and avoid making decisions that might upset or exclude anyone. By being considerate by ensuring that everyone has a good time and keeps the fun going all night.

Leave your friends and end up making new ones - Intentionally leaving your friends to make new ones can be a bit of a letdown for the ones you're out with. Although meeting new people and socialising on a night out can be enjoyable, it's important not to disregard the people you're out with, as they are the ones who care about you and will look out for you.

Camera crazy - Nights out are usually a good time for taking photos as everyone looks their best and feels great. However, it's easy to go overboard and become the group's paparazzi, which can get irritating, especially if some individuals are just trying to relax and enjoy the night.

Order a round of shots, nobody asked for - Don't underestimate the power of shots. If the group isn't interested in taking them, don't get annoyed. They may already be hitting their limit, and one more shot could ruin their night.

Negative Form

Negative Form - All of these actions can have an impact on everyone's night, with some potentially carrying on into the morning and resulting in a bad hangover or worse. These are list of avoidables.

On your ones - Getting lost on a night out can be a real buzzkill. You're out to have fun, not to play a game of hide-and-seek. Plus, wandering aimlessly means missing out on all the action and potentially falling victim to questionable choices. Most of the time it's your friends who end up having to track you down. It's like a never-ending game of cat and mouse.

Roaming the streets alone outside of bars and clubs can be dangerous, especially when you've had a few too many. Drunks can be easy targets for those with bad intentions, so it's important to stick with your group and stay safe.

If you have a tendency to get lost, it's always a good idea to share your phone location with your friends, it might also come in handy if you lose your phone and need to track it down.

Sickness – If you get sick during a night out, it's a signal to call it a night. Drinking too much and too fast can upset your stomach. Take it as a sign to slow down. One tell-tale sign that you're about to be sick is the speed at which your saliva returns after swallowing.

If you're fortunate enough to recover after throwing up stealthily in the toilet or a bush, and have the ability to stay out. Rehydrate yourself and take it slow after that. It's essential to rehydrate and take it easy. It's never a problem to let your friends know that you've had enough. Your friends should always respect your decision to slow down or call it a night.

Bull in a china shop – losing your self-awareness can lead to crashing into people on and off the dance floor, which is never fun. No one wants to be pushed around or accidentally elbowed in the face.

If you accidentally bump into someone, it's important to apologise as this will diffuse any potential conflict. The best thing to do is to stop drinking and try to sober up before you lose complete control.

Closing the night early – If your friends are ending the night early to prioritise your health, it's a sign that you may have had too much to drink and becoming a risk. Even if you feel okay, keep in mind that your friends are cutting their night short due to your condition.

Teammate down – If you find yourself being carried out of the club like a soldier wounded in battle due to excessive drinking, then it's safe to say you've reached your limit. Being carried out by your friends is also not a good look.

If you're the one causing your friends to cut the night short to take care of you, they still love you. But let's face it, being the "designated sick friend" isn't exactly a winning title.

Losing items – Losing personal items on a night out can be a real hassle, especially if you accidentally leave them behind at a venue. To avoid misplacing your belongings, don't take too much out with you - just the bare essentials. Also be mindful of where you place them. Taking these simple precautions can minimize the risk of losing something important on a night out.

Most smart phones can be tracked via the internet, which can be a lifesaver if you misplace them on a night out, by logging into the online portal, you may be able to see its last known location. You can also buy trackers for your other items like your keys, wallet or bag.

Severe Negative Form

Severe Negative Form - these actions carry a significant risk of injury and could result in consequences that last far beyond a typical hangover.

Getting into fights – Fighting is a mood killer for everyone involved. Remember, it takes two to tango, so whether you're the one who instigated the conflict or the one who reacted to someone's nonsense. Arguing or throwing punches at someone is like being back on a playground. There's nothing cool about that and it's just unnecessary drama that will plague the rest of the night, even if you have fully calmed down.

Conflicts can often be defused with patience and understanding, so taking a step back and walking away from a tense situation will help prevent it from escalating.

Getting kicked out for being too drunk – You have definitely lost it if you're finding yourself getting kicked out of a bar or a club for being too drunk. While it may be disappointing to have your night cut short, it's important to remember that the bouncers are likely doing it for your own safety.

It's very important to assess the situation and know if you're still in control. If you come out the club on your own, it's quite possible you might find yourself getting into trouble or hurting yourself. In these situations, it's best to contact your friends to find you immediately. The more drunk you are, the greater at risk you are on your own.

Getting banned – Whatever you did, we wouldn't recommend doing it again. If you find yourself banned from a bar or a club, it's important to take responsibility for your actions and understand that what you did to earn the ban was likely unacceptable behaviour. While it may be tempting to try and fight the ban or sneak back in, it's better to accept the consequences and move on.

Stay Safe While You're Out: Essential Tips for a Perfect Night Out

- Avoid mixing different types of alcohol, such as beer and wine.

- Eat a good-sized meal before going out and avoid only eating light snacks and small treats.

- Be responsible with shots and understand that they can have a strong impact on your body.

- Never leave your drink unattended to avoid the risk of being spiked.

- Know your limits and don't push yourself to drink more than you can handle.

- Don't try to drink away your stresses, as alcohol can have negative effects on your mental health.

- If you weren't feeling your best a few nights before, be aware that your body may not be ready to handle alcohol as usual.

- Sharing your phone's location with friends can help you locate each other in case someone gets separated or lost during a night out.

- Drinking water throughout the night can help you stay hydrated.

- It's important to pay attention to the alcohol percentage listed on the bottle, as consuming stronger alcohol in the same quantities as lower strengths can have a greater effect on your body.

- Ask for help: If you're feeling overwhelmed or unsafe, don't hesitate to ask for help. You can approach security personnel, bartenders or staff to ask for assistance.

- Seek medical attention if you or your friends look or act unwell due to alcohol.

Reviewing The Lists

The 1-2-3 Scale

A helpful way to gauge your level of intoxication. At levels 1 and 2, you're generally in a safe and moderate drinking zone. However, once you reach level 3, your body may start to feel the effects of heavy drinking, and it's a good idea to be more cautious. At this point, your friends may also be more likely to step in and make sure you stay safe. By keeping track of your alcohol intake using this scale, you can make sure you have a fun night without putting your health at risk.

After a night out you should know the whereabouts of where you sit on the scale, the morning after is also a good indication of how far you went. With stage three being so recognisable, stages one and two normally generate Good Form.

Forms

Positive Form - Refers to the typical activities that occur during a night out with friends, such as dancing, socialising, and enjoying good food and drinks. These actions are often spontaneous and unplanned. We like Positive Form!

Questionable Form - May leave you with regrettable decisions or something that might follow you into the morning. Having two or more from our list of Questionable Form would put you into that category, even though this isn't a bad thing, it can reflect on your character.

Negative Form - Unfortunately anything from either the negative or severe list would be an indication that the night might be coming to the end, and it can be difficult to bounce back from. Even one single Negative Form action can ruin the energy for everyone you're out with.

Combine Your Results

Identify where you fall on the 1-2-3 scale, and what your overall Form was on the night out. Use the next page to see what tier of Form your graded in currently.

How Was Your Form?

Good Form

You don't have to drink to have fun on a night out. We don't judge the blue scale if that's what you choose. Alcohol is not for everybody, or maybe you're having a night off. Just make sure to have a good time. The list below starts off well, but only gets worse.

Positive Form

What a successful night out for sure. You had a good understanding of your limits and left no trail of negativity.

Average Form

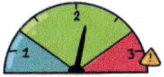

Questionable Form

You consumed your appropriate level of alcohol, but you chose to create a problem to fix in the morning.

Positive Form

It's common to have that "one too many", be aware of what you're drinking and don't ignore the alcohol percentages on the bottle.

Bad Form

Negative Form

Something doesn't quite match here. Something strange must have happened. Not sure you can entirely blame the booze.

Questionable Form

You might be drinking too much and losing control of your actions. You're likely to wake up and think, "Oh, for f***'s sake!"

Negative Form

Dialling back on your drinking will lead to a noticeable change in your actions. It's never too late to turn your Form around.

The Form Book

PARTY HOLIDAYS AND RETIREMENT

The final section of the book covers partying abroad with your friends. Whether you're hitting up bars and clubs or soaking in the local culture, going on an international party holiday is a best chance to create lasting memories with your closest companions. While it may end up being the priciest week of your life in terms of expenses, the excitement and enjoyment you'll experience will make every penny worth it.

Having trustworthy friends who will look after you is essential when traveling abroad for party holidays. It's important to stay safe and out of trouble. To help with this, we've included a list of must-knows and must-have items to bring along - these items can make a huge difference in ensuring a fun and safe experience while abroad.

On a party holiday day, the biggest difference from an average British night out is the extended duration of the drinking, which can be up to three times longer and often starts earlier in the day. Pacing yourself is crucial in this scenario, but it's important to keep in mind that the sun's heat can be just as dehydrating as alcohol. So make sure to stock up on plenty of water throughout the day and drink it regularly.

All Good Things Come To End
Going out and socialising can be fun and far more frequent in young adulthood, but all good things come to an end. Retirement from the night out scene isn't always permanent and happens to all of us at some point.

There is no specific age when you should stop going out, as it varies from person to person. You will eventually reach a point where you realise that full-time clubbing is no longer for you, and it may become a part-time or occasional activity.

Going International

Single's are doubles, double's are quadruple measures. This is why International nights take twice the skill of a typical night out. You might also find that drinks are handed out on entry to the club as an incentive to go in. Another tactic used on the strip abroad is "all you can drink before 11pm". The plastic cup you are given for drinks typically only holds between 200-300ml of liquid, so you will certainly be heading to the bar quite frequently. In the daytime hours you might find the dancefloor pretty vacant at this stage of the night.

The term that gets thrown around a lot is a "Lads Holiday". A group between 4 to 10 lads will head to the strips abroad to party. A "Lads holiday" can also be known as a "Lasses Holiday", which is an all-girl group with the same intentions. Both lads and lasses will likely be aged between 18 to 30, with most of the group's objective being to meet new people. These holidays aren't exclusive to single-sex groups though as good groups of friends and couples fly for the vibes.

Party vibe holidays have been a big part of British culture since the late 60s and over time, have evolved to build the international drinking culture for foreign countries.

The average person normally will only go between 1-3 times on a full party trip in a lifetime as these trips are quite expensive, but also very taxing on you. The vibe is party all day and night, sleep is for the sun beds and power naps between activity's. The itinerary consists of pool parties, beach parties and late nights on the strip, sometimes all on the same day,

An average week in the sun will have you potentially spending between €100 - €230 a day on your activities, drinks and meals. In most cases that in total will be more than the flight and hotel cost. Prices will vary by where you go and what board you choose. Definitely choose bed and breakfast if you want to try restaurants and be as spontaneous as possible, this way you won't find yourself missing meals you have already paid for. Your holiday will be more exciting if you go out and experience local restaurants.

Here's A Cost Breakdown,

Pools drinks - €25 (€5 a drink)
Lunch – €23
Snack - €12
Dinner - €25
Pres - €15
Club drinks - €50 (drinks and entry)

This €150 is an example of the spend on a pool day and a club night out, this is could be classed as tame to some groups! It really varies trip by trip bases (Location and group size being the main factors).

A few ideal places to party are Ibiza, Maga, Kavos, Zante, Malia and Ayia Napa. All these locations vary on how commercialised they are and the ir reputation for drinking culture.

To get the best experience of an abroad trip, go away with your closest friends who will know how to look after you and themselves whilst you're away. There's nothing worse than a lost or injured mate abroad. Knowing everyone inside and out can stop un-necessary arguments and will increases the chance of it becoming the ultimate trip.

Keep Yourself Safe And Know Your Facts
Have all the information
- First Aid (if you get injured)
- Hotel name and number (if you get lost)
- Mates number on paper (if you lose your phone)
- Taxi
- Police

Items to take
- Chest bag (minimises pickpockets)
- Lockable bag (for important items like passport and wallet)
- Emergency funds (card/cash for real emergencies)
- Medications (paracetamol and diarrhoea tablets).

Retirement

Retirement from the party scene can be a significant event in someone's life. It could be a natural progression of aging and settling down, or it could be a result of a significant life change, such as having a child, taking on new responsibilities, or even a change in personal priorities.

However, just because someone retires from the party scene, it doesn't mean they are retiring from socialising or having fun. Some may choose to retire to focus on their career or education, while others may simply prefer a more low-key lifestyle.

Retirement from partying can also be temporary for some individuals. For instance, there may be a friend who disappears into a relationship for a while before resurfacing and hitting the dance floor once again. Someone may retire for a few years, only to come back later with a new perspective and appreciation for the nightlife scene.

For those who choose to retire from the party scene permanently, it can be a time to reflect on the memories and experiences they had during their time in the scene.

Ultimately, whether retirement from the party scene is a temporary or permanent choice, it doesn't have to signify the end of having fun and socialising. Life is full of new experiences and opportunities, and it's up to each individual to find their own way to enjoy it.

Note From The Author:

Dear Reader,

As you come to the end of this book, I leave you with a reminder that Bad Form can always be turned around and used as a tool for growth. Enjoy your nights out and keep in mind the actions you can take to foster Good Form!

Take care of your mates and cherish the memories of the good times you have shared together. And with that, I bid you farewell and raise a glass to your next adventure.

Until next time,

KYLE LIGHTNING

Index

Printed in Great Britain
by Amazon